DECADES OF THE
20TH CENTURY

The 1950s

From the Korean War to Elvis

Stephen Feinstein

Enslow Publishers, Inc.
40 Industrial Road   PO Box 38
Box 398   Aldershot
Berkeley Heights, NJ 07922 Hants GU12 6BP
USA   UK

http://www.enslow.com

Library of Congress Cataloging-in-Publication Data

Feinstein, Stephen.
      The 1950s from the Korean War to Elvis / Stephen
Feinstein.
            p. cm. — (Decades of the 20th century)
      Includes bibliographical references and index.
      Summary: Traces the events, trends, and important people
of the 1950s, including science, technology, politics, fashion,
the arts, sports, and entertainment.
      ISBN 0-7660-1427-4
      1. United States—Civilization—1945——Juvenile literature.
2. Nineteen fifties—Juvenile literature. [1. United States—
Civilization—1945– 2. Nineteen fifties.] I. Title.
E169.12 .F447 2000
973.92—dc21

                              00-008295

Printed in the United States of America

10 9 8 7 6 5 4 3

To Our Readers:
We have done our best to make sure all Internet addresses in this
book were active and appropriate when we went to press.
However, the author and the publisher have no control over and
assume no liability for the material available on those Internet
sites or on other Web sites they may link to. Any comments or
suggestions can be sent by e-mail to comments@enslow.com or
to the address on the back cover.

Illustration Credits: Archive Photos, pp. 11, 50; Bert Randolph
Sugar, *The Great Baseball Players from McGraw to Mantle* (Mineola,
N.Y.: Dover Publications, Inc., 1997), pp. 1, 28, 29; Corel Corporation,
p. 33; Courtesy of Dick Clark Productions, Inc., pp. 25, 58;
Courtesy of the Toaster Museum Foundation, www.toaster.org, p. 7;
Dwight D. Eisenhower Library, pp. 36, 42, 43; Enslow Publishers,
Inc., pp. 6, 16, 17, 20, 54, 57; Express Newspapers/C54/Archive
Photos, p. 27; JoAnne Olian, ed., *Everyday Fashions of the Forties,
As Pictured in Sears Catalogs* (New York: Dover Publications, Inc.,
1992), pp. 1, 12, 13, 21; John F. Kennedy Library, p. 49;
Levittown Public Library, pp. 8–9; Library of Congress, pp. 1, 2,
3, 14, 15, 22, 26, 32, 34, 44, 45, 47, 59, 60, 61; March of Dimes
Birth Defects Foundation, p. 56; *Movie Star Postcards* (New York:
Dover Publications, Inc., 1986), pp. 18, 23, 60; National
Aeronautics and Space Administration, pp. 53, 55; National
Archives, pp. 1, 2, 4, 5, 37, 38, 39, 40, 41, 60; Photofest, p. 24;
Photo Stanley A. Bauman, p. 31; Reproduced from the *Dictionary
of American Portraits*, Published by Dover Publications, Inc., in
1967, p. 3, 61; Unisys Corporation, p. 52.

Cover Illustrations: Corel Corporation; Dwight D. Eisenhower
Library; Library of Congress; *Movie Star Postcards* (New York:
Dover Publications, Inc., 1986); National Aeronautics and Space
Administration; National Archives.

Every effort has been made to locate the copyright owners of the
pictures used in this book. If due acknowledgment has not been
made, we sincerely regret the omission.

Contents

The decade of the 1950s was a time of great change in American life. In 1945, a victorious United States had emerged from World War II as the wealthiest, most powerful nation on Earth. America entered a period of growth and prosperity that would last throughout the 1950s. Jobs were plentiful. More Americans could realize the American dream—a home of their own, perhaps in one of the new suburbs springing up all over the country.

On the one hand, life was good. Americans had many happy hours of family togetherness, either on family vacations or at home, huddled around their television sets. On the other hand, something was very wrong. Americans' fear of the Soviet Union and communism resulted in family fallout shelters, Senator Joseph McCarthy's campaign of intimidation against those he accused of having Communist "sympathies," the Korean War, and the building of a huge nuclear arsenal. The 1950s would go down in history as a decade of sharp contrasts and unique happenings.

The 1950s were seriously affected by the scientific advances of the previous decade, especially the atomic bomb. After the United States used the atomic bomb (opposite) in Japan to end World War II, the Cold War began. The Soviet Union was racing to build weapons as dangerous as those of the United States. As a result, Americans of the 1950s often lived in fear of the possibility of nuclear war.

Early in the 1950s, Americans, still weary from World War II, entered yet another war—this one in Korea, where the United States hoped to drive the Communist North Koreans from South Korea. At left, members of the 24th Infantry Regiment arrive to fight in July 1950.

5

The American Dream

In contrast to the years of economic hardship during the Great Depression of the 1930s and the strict rationing of goods during the years of World War II, the 1950s were a time of consumerism. A consumer-oriented lifestyle was developing among the rapidly growing middle class. All sorts of things were now available to Americans. Many people now had money to spend on television sets and household appliances such as refrigerators, dishwashers, and washing machines. Americans by the millions also bought cars. And the ultimate goal of the American dream—home ownership—was now also within reach of a great many Americans.

Americans and Their Automobiles

In a television commercial, Dinah Shore sang, "See the U.S.A. in Your Chevrolet." And Americans set out to do just that. General Motors' Chevrolet was one of the most popular cars during the 1950s. By the end of the decade, there were no fewer than forty-six different Chevrolet models available.

Automobile manufacturers sent a loud and clear message to Americans: Cars are fun—and it is fun to drive! Americans heard the message and bought far more cars than in any previous period. Especially popular were big, long cars with tail fins.

America during the 1950s was a very prosperous place. The many industrial products that had been needed to fight World War II in the 1940s had created a boom in the economy. Many Americans could now afford to live well, and they took advantage of it, buying all sorts of new appliances (above) and other luxury items.

People drove everywhere—to the suburban shopping malls, to their jobs, to drive-in fast-food stands, to drive-in movies, to visit friends and relatives, to explore the next state, or to visit the nation's fabulous parklands. Often they drove just for the sake of driving—to enjoy the feeling of movement along the open road in their new cars (opposite).

By 1952, there were already more than 52 million cars on the roads across America. Traffic congestion was becoming a problem. There simply were not enough roads to handle the increasing amount of traffic. So in 1956, Congress passed the National Defense Highway Act, in part to be able to move armed forces quickly around the country if necessary. The law would build a nationwide system of interstate freeways. The planned 42,500 miles of divided highway, which took decades to complete, would eventually link every major city in the country.

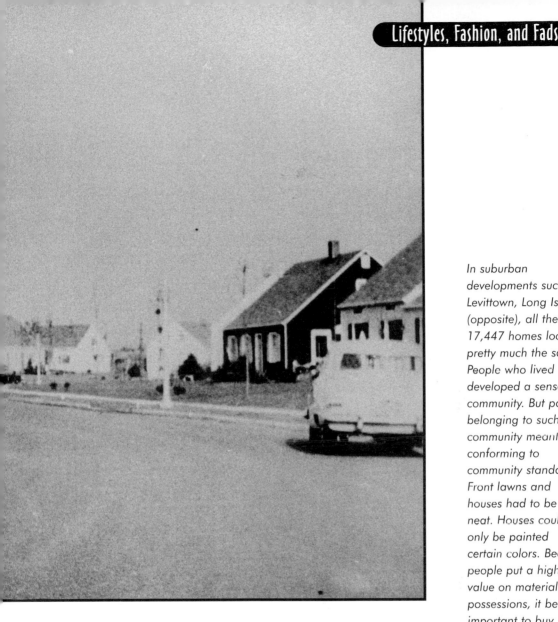

The Suburbs

In the 1950s, those who had achieved the ultimate goal of the American dream were living in the best of all possible worlds—the American suburbs. At least, that is how it must have seemed to those who had yet to attain this goal. Suburban middle-class American family life was glowingly portrayed each night on television as the epitome of easy living.

In suburban developments such as Levittown, Long Island (opposite), all the 17,447 homes looked pretty much the same. People who lived there developed a sense of community. But part of belonging to such a community meant conforming to community standards. Front lawns and houses had to be kept neat. Houses could only be painted certain colors. Because people put a high value on material possessions, it became important to buy whatever home appliances one's neighbors had and to drive a new car to keep one's status. If financial or other problems prevented a family from "keeping up with the Joneses" next door, the result was often extreme frustration and unhappiness.

9

Conformity extended beyond the floor plans of suburban homes to fashion. Men wore gray flannel suits (opposite), considered the appropriate "uniform" for a successful American businessman.

The Man in the Gray Flannel Suit

The new American suburban lifestyle was characterized by conformity in external appearances as well as in personal goals, opinions, and values. Not only did the streets and houses look the same, but so did the styles of clothing. The typical suburban employee of a big corporation, who came to be called an "organization man," commuted to work in the city. He wore a gray flannel suit or some equally conservative "uniform" to work. He kept his hair short. He usually wore a narrow-brimmed hat while traveling to and from work.

The organization man's job was important to him—whether he liked his work or not. He liked the suburban lifestyle it let him lead.

Black Turtlenecks and Beatniks

Some suburbanites eventually rejected what they considered the hollow values of the suburbs and the corporate world. Others were also turned off by the growing conformity they believed would stifle creativity in American life. Known as Beatniks, these people—among them writer Jack Kerouac and poet Allen Ginsberg—rejected the culture of materialism and the conformity of organization men. They valued experience more than things, spontaneity more than routine. They challenged commonly held notions about how people should live, work, and play. Jack Kerouac set out on the road,

crisscrossing America many times and even traveling through Mexico, in search of adventure and freedom. His 1957 novel, *On the Road*, is a fictional account of his experiences.

The Beat lifestyle typically involved sexual freedom and the use of drugs such as marijuana and alcohol. The Beatniks could be seen hanging out in coffeehouses. They listened to jazz music and Beat poetry. Of course, not one of them would be wearing gray flannel—or any other kind of suit. Many of the men, however, wore a different uniform: black turtleneck sweaters, blue jeans, and sandals. Beatnik women typically wore black leotards and short skirts. Apparently, even those who rejected corporate ideas were not immune to conformity of some sort.

"Truly Feminine Women"

Throughout the 1950s, women were often portrayed in magazines and advertisements as domestic servants whose main duty was catering to the needs of their husbands and children. According to *Life* magazine, a "truly feminine" woman's proper place was in the home, especially the kitchen.

In real life, however, more women were beginning to work outside the home in the 1950s. They had little time to prepare elaborate meals. By 1956, 32 percent of all women were part of the American labor force. Unfortunately, most women had to work at low-paying clerical, assembly-line, or service jobs. Only a small number of women held

Women, like their husbands, wanted to follow a very particular fashion style in the 1950s. Most wore feminine, yet tailored dresses (below), which were convenient for those who continued to work outside the home.

While older women dressed in professional-looking, tailored clothing, young ladies wore some unusual outfits in the 1950s. One of the most memorable symbols of the decade is the teenage girl in a poodle skirt with a crinolin slip, and a pair of saddle shoes (opposite).

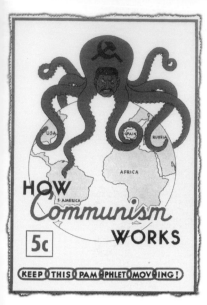

HOW *Communism* WORKS

5¢

KEEP THIS PAMPHLET MOVING!

During the early years of the Cold War, Americans began to develop a deep-seated fear of communism and the Soviet Union that hoped to spread its government system to other places around the world. This 1938 pamphlet (above) shows the fearful attitude with which Americans regarded the Communist threat. Such attitudes were even more apprehensive by the 1950s, after the development of nuclear weapons.

management positions or practiced a profession. When women went into the kitchen after a hard day's work, they were likely to heat up frozen TV dinners for their families.

Although women's roles were changing, the most popular fashions of the 1950s emphasized women's femininity and sexuality. By 1950, Christian Dior's "New Look" had become the height of fashion. Dior's clothing enhanced a woman's natural curves, creating the classic hourglass figure—skintight tailoring around the bosom, a narrow waist, and a full skirt that often flared out. Stiletto heels were popular, and women did not feel completely dressed until they had painted their lips bright red. The well-dressed woman often wore a hat in public. Career women, dressed in suits, always wore gloves.

The Cold War: The Era of Duck and Cover

But there was more going on in the 1950s than interesting fashions. In September 1949, Americans learned that their Cold War adversary, the Soviet Union, had built an atomic bomb. America was no longer the only nation with nuclear weapons. To Americans, the world had suddenly become much more dangerous. Soon, air-raid drills were being conducted across the country. When the siren sounded, people were to go to the nearest air-raid shelter and stay there until they heard the all-clear siren.

Even schoolchildren participated in air-raid drills. At the sound of the siren, teachers shouted, "Take cover!" The children would immediately follow the "duck-and-cover" routine they had been taught: They would get under their desks and put their head between their knees and their hands over their head. They were warned not to look at the window, because they would be blinded by the flash of the nuclear explosion.

Although Americans were terrified of what could happen to them in a nuclear war, it is doubtful that many took the civil defense drills seriously. People were well aware of the incredible destruction that resulted from an atomic bomb. So when people were told to stay indoors, or to avoid looking at the window, they had good reason to wonder how these measures could save them.

Still, there were many who believed they could survive a nuclear attack if they had access to a bomb shelter. Some Americans bought their own family shelters, which were installed in their backyards. Those who bought fallout shelters believed they were preventing the American dream from turning into the American nightmare.

Many Americans were so fearful that a nuclear war could take place at any moment that they erected bomb shelters (above) in their backyards. Stocked with food and supplies, many people believed the bomb shelters could help them survive the many long months or even years of devastation after a nuclear war. Family shelters, designed by Walter Kidde Nuclear Laboratories, sold for $3,000, and an economy model was available for $2,500.

15

Popular Fads and Pastimes

Americans in the 1950s were caught up in many popular fads. Perhaps to take their minds off the looming threats to America's security, people were enthusiastic about whatever seemed to be fun. College students could be seen stuffing themselves into telephone booths and cars, as if conducting serious research into the number of people that could fit into a small space. Some people stared in fascination as wire coils called Slinkies walked down flights of stairs. Some played with globs of moldable silicone called Silly Putty. Others tossed Frisbees.

Perhaps the most popular fad of the decade was the Hula-Hoop, first introduced in 1958 by Arthur Melin and Richard Knerr of Wham-O Manufacturing. By 1959, millions of young Americans were swinging Hula-Hoops around their hips, and soon, Hula-Hoop contests were being held all around the country.

The Hula-Hoop and Slinky craze (opposite and below) spread throughout much of the world. But the Soviets were not buying it, scorning the Hula-Hoop as an example of "the emptiness of American culture."

Young Rebels

In 1955, *Rebel Without a Cause* became a big hit with American teenagers. They identified with the film's young star, James Dean, who blamed his parents for his state of confusion and anguish. Many teens in the 1950s, especially those growing up in suburbs, were bored by the blandness of their surroundings. They were confused by society's standards and expectations for them, and resentful of adults' lack of understanding.

After the great success of movies such as The Wild One, starring Marlon Brando (opposite), it became "cool" to wear a black leather jacket and act tough. Teens who did so became known as greasers. Some greasers joined youth gangs, which were often seen as a threat to conservative adults.

Fictional characters showing the concerns of 1950s teenagers appeared in literature as well as in film. Teen readers found their spokesman in Holden Caulfield, the teenage hero of J. D. Salinger's novel *The Catcher in the Rye* (1951). Holden Caulfield shared their frustration with the hypocrisy of adult values.

In 1954, the young actor Marlon Brando starred in *The Wild One*. In the film, he played the leader of a motorcycle gang. The movie inspired young people who identified with the bikers' desire to test the limits of society's tolerance for delinquent behavior. While young people related to the film's heroes, older Americans were becoming concerned with the problems of juvenile delinquency and gang-related crime. Movies such as *The Blackboard Jungle* (1955) pointed out the ugly behavior of unruly youth in New York City's schools.

Creatures From Outer Space

As if Americans in the 1950s did not have enough to worry about with nuclear weapons, there was something new to fear—an invasion from outer space! Hollywood produced a number of science-fiction films dealing with extraterrestrial visitors, such as *War of the Worlds* (1953) and *Invasion of the Body Snatchers* (1956).

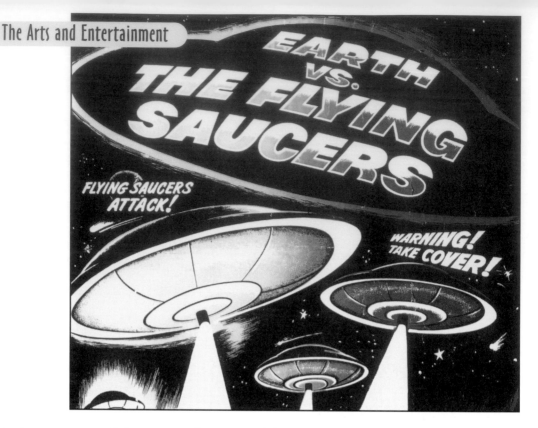

Despite the sometimes drab conformity Americans of the 1950s showed in fashion and in their choices to live in suburbs, they seemed to enjoy films that depicted far-fetched, fantastic events (above).

Many people were either thrilled or horrified by the antics of space creatures on the big screen. Others reported seeing "flying saucers"—strange lights in the night skies over America. Nobody could prove whether the UFOs (unidentified flying objects), as the lights came to be called, were real—perhaps visitors from another planet—or just a figment of people's imagination.

New Ideas in the Movies

Movie producers in the 1950s were afraid that Americans would be so fascinated by television and all the entertainment they could enjoy in their own living rooms, that they would forget to go to the movies. So the movie industry came up with new ideas to attract an audience. They began to use a wide-screen process known as CinemaScope, often presenting biblical spectacles with casts of thousands—films such as *The Ten Commandments* (1956) and *Ben-Hur* (1959).

Producers also made movies that gave the illusion of three dimensions. In 3-D horror films such as *House of Wax* (1953), *It Came from Outer Space* (1953), and *Creature from the Black Lagoon* (1954), the illusion of depth was so vivid that moviegoers would often duck as things seemed to leap off the screen and into their laps. There was only one catch—in order to experience the third dimension, moviegoers had to wear special glasses. Many people found these glasses annoying. Some even reported getting headaches.

TV Westerns and Millions of Little Cowboys

Along with sitcoms and variety shows, Westerns were among the most popular television shows of the 1950s. Galloping across the screen were popular cowboys such as Hopalong Cassidy, the Lone Ranger, the Cisco Kid, Roy Rogers, and Gene Autry. Westerns especially appealed to children, who spent long hours in front of the television, riding along with their favorite heroes. Before long, millions of young children were prowling the streets of America, wearing big cowboy hats and firing their toy cap guns at each other in mock gunfights. By the mid-1950s, more sophisticated Westerns such as *Gunsmoke* and *Have Gun Will Travel* were being made. These shows became popular mainly with adult audiences.

Programs such as The Lone Ranger appealed to children as well as adults. The popularity of Westerns even caused a fashion trend among young boys, who dressed in cowboy hats and fringed shirts like their favorite television stars (below). However, when Walt Disney began broadcasting his Davy Crockett series, children were captivated by the famous "King of the Wild Frontier." Millions traded in their cowboy hats for Davy Crockett "coonskin" caps, but kept their cap guns ready in their holster belts.

Comedy Comes to TV

Television sitcoms such as Leave It to Beaver, Ozzie and Harriet, Father Knows Best, and I Love Lucy (below) presented a world in which everyone lived in harmony and liked each other. Parents never raised their voices in anger. The happy characters easily solved any minor problem. Real problems such as poverty, crime, and alcohol or drug addiction did not exist in this ideal world.

Television was so popular in the 1950s in part because it was still a novelty to most American families. It also provided a form of entertainment that appealed to a broad range of people. It quickly became a main source of family entertainment. Millions of homes throughout America were filled with the sounds of laughter, thanks to wildly popular television comedians such as Lucille Ball, Jackie Gleason, and Milton "Uncle Miltie" Berle, known as Mr. Television.

Marilyn Monroe and the Sexual Revolution

The sexual revolution that would erupt in America in the 1960s was starting to simmer in the 1950s. Perhaps the one person who best symbolized Americans' fantasies and notions about sexuality in the 1950s was Marilyn Monroe. Born Norma Jean Mortenson in 1926, Monroe grew up to become a screen sensation during the 1950s. She starred in such films as *Gentlemen Prefer Blondes* (1953), *How to Marry a Millionaire* (1953), and *Some Like It Hot* (1959). Marilyn Monroe did indeed have a beautiful face and body, but she was also a fine actress and singer, and she put her comedic skills to good use by satirizing the Hollywood sex goddess role that made her famous.

Despite her worldwide fame and image as a sex symbol, Marilyn Monroe (above) was not as successful in her personal life. Her marriage to baseball star Joe DiMaggio ended in divorce, as did her marriage to playwright Arthur Miller. In 1962, she committed suicide at the age of thirty-six.

Rock 'n' Roll

In his hit rock 'n' roll song "Roll Over Beethoven," singer Chuck Berry told Beethoven, who symbolized classical music, to "roll over." He might just as well have also advised every other older musical style to "roll over" and get out of the way—because rock 'n' roll was here to stay. Due to its almost instant popularity among America's teens, rock 'n' roll swept aside all other forms of music.

Rock 'n' roll did not just appear overnight. It was based on a combination of black blues and R&B (rhythm and blues), and white blues, or "hillbilly" music. What these kinds of music had in common was their soulful expression of raw emotion. Rock 'n'

roll was a huge success because it had a winning formula—simple melodies, basic chords, and a backbeat. It was loud and sexy. There was nothing subtle about it. And it was great to dance to, as seen on Dick Clark's television show *American Bandstand*. An added benefit of rock 'n' roll was that older Americans, including the parents of teenagers, hated it. When young Americans went crazy over rock 'n' roll, the older generation reacted with alarm, fearing that the music was wildly sexual and would lead young people astray. So millions of American teens, especially those with a rebellious streak, became devoted fans of 1950s rock stars such as Jerry Lee Lewis, Buddy Holly, Chuck Berry, Little Richard, and Fats Domino. The biggest rock 'n' roll sensation was Elvis Presley, who came to be called the King of Rock 'n' Roll.

Rock 'n' roll was able to succeed in part because there were so many young people to enjoy it. A post–World War II baby boom led to such a high birthrate that, by 1958, one third of America's population was under the age of fifteen. This new generation of Americans, who came to be known as baby boomers, would eventually create a new youth culture based on rock 'n' roll music.

Dick Clark's successful television program, American Bandstand (above), was popular because it showcased the latest songs and musicians. It was also a hit with teenagers because it included lots of dancing. By watching (or participating in) the show, teenagers could learn the newest dance steps.

Elvis Presley (opposite), one of the most popular rock singers, became known as the King of Rock 'n' Roll.

Jazz—Some Like It Cool

True jazz fans in the 1950s were not about to give up the music they loved. While rock 'n' roll got hotter, jazz became cool—real cool. In previous decades, jazz had been widely popular, mainly because people liked to dance to it. But by the 1950s, the most interesting and innovative jazz was not dance music, and the audience for it was much smaller. Fans enjoyed listening to the brilliant, intricate improvisations of musicians such as Miles Davis, Theolonious Monk, Dizzy Gillespie, Sonny Rollins, John Coltrane, and McCoy Tyner. The music had become serious, and it required concentration on the part of listeners. Audiences would sit quietly in rapt attention while the cool sounds of the Modern Jazz Quartet wafted over them.

Dizzy Gillespie (above) introduced new forms of jazz that were inspired by Afro-Cuban rhythms. In 1956, Gillespie and his band had the unique honor of becoming the first band ever sponsored by the United States Department of State in an international tour.

Rebels With Paint

What if an artist set out to create art specifically to outrage and shock people? And what if the intended audience not only refused to be offended but took an interest in the new kind of art? This is what happened in the art world during the 1950s.

Painters who, like the Beatniks, rejected conformity and materialism, were determined to rebel against limits on how they could paint. The first step in eliminating boundaries was to do away with the subject—there would be no recognizable image. Paintings, which tended to be huge, were abstract, and artists such as Jackson

Pollock became known as abstract expressionists. In a sense, abstract expressionist paintings were often about the act of painting itself. Pollock devised a way to drip paint onto huge canvases stretched out on the floor. Others attacked the canvas, lunging with a knife or trowel. Active painters such as these were called Action Painters.

Art lovers at first were mostly baffled by the displays of blobs, drips, and scribbles. But gradually, the public came to accept and value the paintings of the would-be rebels. And within a few years, abstract expressionist paintings were not only hanging in art galleries and museums, but could also be seen decorating the walls of corporate offices.

Action painting, as the works of Jackson Pollock were often called, stunned many people at first. Soon, however, even the strait-laced businesspeople of the 1950s (above) began to enjoy the wild new technique.

27

The Brooklyn Dodgers— "Bums" No Longer

Brooklyn Dodger fans were certainly among the most loyal and devoted fans in the history of baseball. Most likely, the perception of the Dodgers as a perpetual underdog helped stir up the passion of the fans, who affectionately referred to their favorite team as "dem Bums," in the local Brooklyn accent. Time and time again, the Brooklyn Dodgers would come close to winning the World Series. And each time they would lose. The Dodgers faced their rivals, the New York Yankees, in the World Series in 1941, 1947, 1949, 1952, and 1953. Each time, the Dodgers lost, even though they had exceptionally fine ball players such as Jackie Robinson, Gil Hodges, Roy Campanella, and Johnny Podres. "Wait till next year," became the theme song of the Brooklyn Dodgers.

But then, in 1955, "Dem Bums" finally defeated the New York Yankees in the World Series! The Brooklyn Dodgers were "Bums" no longer. Unfortunately, the joy was short-lived. In the 1956 World Series, the Dodgers lost to the New York Yankees once again. Then, in 1958, the Brooklyn Dodgers moved away and became the Los Angeles Dodgers. Some fans never forgave "dem Bums" for leaving Brooklyn.

Roy Campanella (opposite) was the first African-American catcher to play in the major leagues, coming to play for the Dodgers in 1948. He proved himself an outstanding player, being named Most Valuable Player three times. Unfortunately, in 1958, Campanella was involved in a serious automobile accident that ended his career and left him in a wheelchair.

First baseman Gil Hodges (below) helped lead his team to five pennant wins. An outstanding hitter, Hodges also showed skill in the field, winning three Golden Glove awards.

Born in Brockton, Massachusetts, Rocky Marciano (opposite, at right, fighting Jersey Joe Walcott in 1952) turned professional in 1947. He went on to become one of the most famous boxers of all time.

Rocky Marciano— Heavyweight Champion of the 1950s

Considered one of the "hardest punchers" in boxing history, Rocky Marciano held the world heavyweight boxing championship title from 1952 to 1956. Born in Massachusetts as Rocco Marchegiano, Marciano won his heavyweight title in September 1952 by defeating Jersey Joe Walcott. Marciano successfully defended his heavyweight title six times. When he retired in 1956, he had won *all* of his forty-nine professional fights.

Ben Hogan: Great American Golfer

In 1953, the Associated Press named golfer Ben Hogan the male athlete of the year. The honor was well earned. Throughout his career, Hogan won more than sixty tournaments. He won the United States Open four times, the Masters twice, the Professional Golfers' Association (PGA) twice, and the British Open once. One of those tournament wins especially showed Hogan's tremendous ability to overcome obstacles. In 1949, Hogan was seriously injured in a car accident. Just seventeen months after the accident, still wearing bandages on his legs, Hogan not only played in the 1950 United States Open, but actually won the tournament!

Althea Gibson: Breaking Barriers in Tennis

For many years, tennis was predominantly a sport for white men, at least professionally. In the 1950s, Althea Gibson changed all that. One of the leading women's amateur players from 1950 to 1958, Gibson became the first well-known African-American tennis player. Among other major victories, Gibson won two consecutive Wimbledon singles titles in 1957 and 1958, as well as the United States Open singles titles in both those years. She was the first African-American player to win these important tournaments.

Born in Silver, South Carolina, in 1927, Althea Gibson (opposite) spent most of her childhood in New York City. After she began playing amateur tennis in the early 1940s, Gibson made great strides both for women and for African Americans. She ended her tennis career in 1958, then went on to become a professional golfer. Her efforts helped open the world of tennis (above) to future African-American players.

The Red Scare

On February 9, 1950, Joseph McCarthy, a Republican senator from Wisconsin, announced that he had a list of 205 Communists who worked in the State Department. If this sensational charge were true, then America was in deep trouble. But in speeches over the next few days, McCarthy was vague when reporters asked for details. His list of 205 names shrank to 57, and then to just 4 names. It was also not clear whether the people named were actually Communists, Communist sympathizers, or people who somehow helped the cause of communism. But details did not seem to matter to the senator, or to many of his listeners.

And so began McCarthy's four-year campaign of accusations and threats. McCarthy had shrewdly concluded that playing on Americans' fears of communism was a good way to win political power. People from Hollywood, the media, politics, and other walks of life were brought before McCarthy's committee and questioned by McCarthy and his faithful assistants—Roy Cohn and G. David Schine.

Many people lost their jobs as a result of McCarthy's activities. Careers were destroyed and lives were wrecked. McCarthy, in a short time, became one of the most powerful and feared men in America. Few of his fellow politicians were willing to speak against him. They knew that many Americans at the time were genuinely afraid of communism.

Americans stood by while McCarthy continued to harass people. But in the fall of 1953, McCarthy finally bit off more than he could chew. He went after the United States Army, claiming he would expose the Communists lurking there.

Although the United States and the Soviet Union had been allies during World War II, soon after the war ended, the two nations began to regard each other as a threat. Relations became so strained that a "Cold War"—a state of hostility that would divide much of the world between loyalty to democratic America and the Communist Soviet Union— began. By the 1950s, the Cold War had grown even more severe. Cartoons (opposite) in America and its non-Communist allies depicted the Soviet menace to freedom around the world.

Representing the army in the controversial Army-McCarthy hearings was attorney Joseph Welch, who successfully refuted all of McCarthy's charges. When Welch could listen no longer to McCarthy's cruel treatment of witnesses, he said, "Have you left no sense of decency?" The hearings, which were televised to large audiences, finally gave Americans a chance to see Joseph McCarthy (above) and his ridiculous behavior and unfair tactics firsthand.

The Army-McCarthy hearings in 1954 were televised daily to an audience of 80 million viewers. On television, Americans saw McCarthy's mean-spirited behavior. This was the beginning of the end for McCarthy. Public opinion turned against him. Later that year, the Senate condemned McCarthy for his behavior. McCarthy lost his influence. He died in May 1957 from complications due to alcoholism.

Atomic Spies

When the Soviet Union exploded an atomic bomb in 1949, Americans were shocked. Americans had assumed that the Soviet Union was far behind the United States in science and technology. It seemed that the only way the Soviets could have built a bomb was by stealing secrets from the United States. And the United States government was determined to expose spies who gave away secrets, and put a stop to nuclear espionage.

In 1950, the Federal Bureau of Investigation (FBI) arrested Julius and Ethel Rosenberg. They had been named as members of a spy ring plotting to pass atomic secrets to the Soviets. The couple claimed they were innocent and would give no further information. The Rosenbergs had been active members of the Communist party during the 1930s but dropped out in 1943, when their first son was born. Ethel's brother, David Greenglass, had confessed to being part of the spy ring. He claimed that he had handed over secret documents to the Rosenbergs.

On March 29, 1951, a jury convicted the Rosenbergs of espionage. And on April 5, Judge Irving Kaufman sentenced them to die in the electric chair. According to Kaufman, the Rosenbergs' crime was "worse than murder." Recent evidence shows that Julius Rosenberg was indeed guilty of spying. His wife, on the other hand, was not, although she knew of her husband's activities.

Many Americans at the time felt that the Rosenbergs' sentence was too harsh. But many others believed the Rosenbergs had received a fair trial. In any case, the government was determined to make an example of them. On June 19, 1953, the Rosenbergs died in the electric chair.

In light of growing anticommunist hysteria during the Red Scare, it was understandable that some Americans would believe that Soviet spies were at work, giving out vital information about America's nuclear know-how. The Rosenbergs (above) were considered dangerous people who were trying to bring about the downfall of the United States.

The Korean War

"We are going to fight!" said President Harry Truman to his daughter, Margaret, on June 25, 1950, on learning that the Communist North Korean Army had just invaded South Korea.

Two days later, Truman, with the approval of the United Nations (UN) Security Council, ordered American military forces to help defend the South Koreans against the Communists. America was at war again, just five years after the end of World War II.

By 1950, it seemed to the United States that the Communist Soviet Union and China were bent on world domination. The "free world"—the United States and its allies—would have to preserve its democratic way of life. When World War II ended in 1945, Korea, which had been occupied by the Japanese, was divided by an agreement between the United States and the Soviet Union. North Korea became a Communist nation under dictator Kim Il Sung. South Korea was ruled by anticommunist dictator Syngman Rhee.

By 1950, the leaders of North and South Korea began boasting that they would unify all of Korea under their own rule. When the Soviet-supported North Korean Army finally invaded the South, the Cold War

Believing in a policy of containment of communism, President Harry Truman thought it was the United States' duty as the leading power of the free world to force the North Korean troops that had invaded South Korea back to their own side of the 38th parallel. In response to the North Korean invasion, Truman signed an order (opposite), sending American troops to fight in Korea.

United Nations (UN) trucks are seen below bringing troops and supplies south of the 38th parallel during the UN's retreat in early 1951. The 38th parallel was the controversial border between North and South Korea. Americans feared crossing it to go after the North Korean troops would encourage China or the Soviet Union to enter the war, which might eventually lead to the use of nuclear weapons.

General Douglas MacArthur, who had achieved fame as Supreme Allied Commander of the Pacific during World War II, led the UN forces in the Korean War. Above, he observes the bombing of Inchon, a successful attack that eventually forced the North Koreans out of South Korea.

reached a boiling point. The North Koreans refused to withdraw. So the United Nations authorized forces, mainly American troops, to push them back.

Once the North Koreans began their invasion, they quickly captured Seoul, the South Korean capital, and pushed deep into the southern part of the country. The situation looked bleak. Then, American General Douglas MacArthur, in charge of the United Nations forces, devised a brilliant but risky strategy. On September 15, 1950, his troops surprised the North Koreans at Inchon, 150 miles behind enemy lines. The North Korean Army was forced to retreat.

General Douglas MacArthur

The war should have ended once the North Koreans left the South. After all, that had been the goal of the United States and United Nations intervention. But now, President Truman, with the encouragement of General

MacArthur, saw an opportunity to invade the North and unite both Koreas under the rule of the South. So the goal was revised.

With the approval of the United Nations, MacArthur's forces pushed northward. MacArthur assured President Truman that there was nothing to worry about—the Chinese would not attack. But suddenly, waves of Chinese troops swept across the border. During the bitterly cold winter of 1950–1951, the American forces suffered high casualties and were driven back to the 38th parallel.

MacArthur came up with another plan. He tried to convince Truman that they could win the war by bombing Chinese air bases in Manchuria. MacArthur would not take no for an answer. The Truman administration thought the most sensible plan was to forget about uniting the two Koreas and to seek a peace agreement that kept the country divided.

When MacArthur heard that Truman was planning to seek a cease-fire, he decided to challenge Truman's strategy. MacArthur spoke out in public, arguing against the president's plans. President Truman, who was MacArthur's Commander in Chief, was furious. Although MacArthur was widely admired by Americans, his conduct was unacceptable. On April 11, 1951, Truman fired MacArthur. The soldier who would not obey orders was relieved of his command.

General Douglas MacArthur (below) remains one of the most controversial military figures in American history. Fired by Truman for insubordination, MacArthur left the army after delivering a famous speech to Congress in which he said, "Old soldiers never die. They just fade away."

Dwight David Eisenhower, the famous general who had led the Allied troops in the D-Day invasion of France, became the thirty-fourth president in 1953. Seen below with his wife, Mamie, Eisenhower did not resemble a military leader when he was president. Instead of issuing stern orders, he was organized, considerate, and very patient.

Few Americans had a negative comment about the conservative presidency of Dwight Eisenhower. He did little to offend most people. Perhaps his greatest flaw was that he often preferred to play golf (opposite) rather than concern himself with executive business. The old general inspired confidence, and he seemed like a nice guy. Supporters took to wearing "I like Ike" buttons.

Eisenhower Becomes President

Peace negotiations in Korea began in July 1951 and continued throughout 1952, but progress was slow. And while the talks went on, fighting continued. Dwight D. Eisenhower, the popular war hero of World War II, was the Republican presidential candidate in the 1952 elections. He promised that, if elected, he would promptly end the war in Korea and make sure that Americans continued to enjoy prosperity at home. Americans liked what they heard. And they liked "Ike," as Eisenhower came to be called.

Adlai Stevenson was the Democrats' candidate. But many Americans felt it was time for a change. There had not been a Republican president in office since Herbert Hoover in the early 1930s. So Americans proved how much they liked Ike by electing him president.

Eisenhower kept his promise to end the Korean War. An armistice was signed on July 27, 1953. There were no winners in Korea. It remained a land divided, as it had been before the war began. North and South Korea were in ruins, their economies destroyed, and both sides had suffered hundreds of thousands of casualties. America had also lost some thirty-four thousand soldiers.

Before he was elected in 1952, Eisenhower expressed his dissatisfaction with the stalemate that had occurred in the Korean War. After MacArthur had forced the North Koreans out of South Korea, little progress had been made toward winning the war. Eisenhower promised to go to Korea, to see the situation for himself. He kept that promise after his election and a truce was finally signed in 1953. Along with his vice president, Richard Nixon (above), Dwight Eisenhower was elected to a second term in office in 1956.

Eisenhower proved to be a popular, although somewhat dull, president. His administration tended to favor the interests of big business. However, Eisenhower was involved in a large expansion of the Social Security system. He worked toward passage of the first civil rights act (1957) since Reconstruction ended in 1877. He also helped provide the first major federal funding for education and established the Department of Health, Education, and Welfare (HEW) as a Cabinet position in 1953. In 1956, voters still liked Ike. They reelected him to four more years in the White House.

Fighting for Civil Rights

For years since the end of the Civil War, African Americans, especially in the South, had to use separate facilities from white Americans—everything from separate rest rooms to separate drinking fountains. Racist whites, who refused to grant blacks the equal rights they had won after the Civil War, referred to this system as "separate but equal."

On May 17, 1954, the United States Supreme Court, in *Brown* v. *Board of Education of Topeka, Kansas*, finally ruled that separate facilities, in regard to education, were inherently unequal. At the time, 40 percent of American public schools were still segregated, or separated by race. The Supreme Court ordered them to be desegregated.

Even so, people's prejudices did not vanish overnight. When African-American students tried to enter what had been all-white schools, they faced the bitter defiance of many Southern whites. For several years, there was very little progress in desegregating schools. Then, in 1957, African Americans in Little Rock, Arkansas, won a court order allowing nine

Since the end of slavery, white Southerners had done all they could to keep African Americans in a state as close to slavery as possible. Among the tactics used by racist whites to "keep blacks in their place" was the Jim Crow system. Jim Crow, or segregation, laws were put in place throughout the South. The laws created separate facilities, such as drinking fountains (below), waiting rooms, and seats in buses, for whites and blacks.

African-American students to enter Little Rock's Central High School. Arkansas Governor Orval Faubus, who opposed school integration, ordered the Arkansas National Guard to block the entrance to the school. For the next three weeks, photos of armed troops preventing the nine students from entering the school appeared in newspapers all across the country. On September 24, 1957, President Eisenhower sent a thousand army troops to Little Rock. On September 25, they made sure the African-American students were allowed into the school.

Rosa Parks and the Montgomery Bus Boycott

Meanwhile, civil rights progress was being made in other areas. On December 1, 1955, Rosa Parks, an African-American seamstress, was riding on a bus in Montgomery, Alabama. When the bus driver ordered her to give up her seat to a white man, she refused, thereby breaking the law. She was arrested, put on trial, convicted, and fined. Inspired by Rosa Parks's courageous act, Dr. Martin Luther King, Jr., and other black civil rights leaders organized a peaceful boycott of Montgomery's bus system. The boycott lasted until December 20, 1956, when the United States Supreme Court ruled that Alabama's bus segregation laws were unconstitutional.

A New Leader for the Soviet Union

Joseph Stalin, the dictator who had ruled the Soviet Union since 1929, died in 1953. Although he had used secret police to terrorize the population and was responsible for the deaths of millions of Soviet citizens, many Soviets mourned his passing.

The new Soviet leader, Nikita Khrushchev, was determined to improve the lives of the Soviet people. After denouncing Stalin's misdeeds in a speech, Khrushchev made it clear that he intended to make reforms. He was in favor of easing the government's strict control of every aspect of life and the official censorship of the arts and media. Under Khrushchev, people began to enjoy a greater degree of freedom to express their views. But while a new day seemed to be dawning at home, the Soviet government maintained its tight grip over the other Communist nations of Eastern Europe.

The Failed Hungarian Revolution

In October 1956, the Hungarian people rose up against the Soviet-backed government in their country. The rebellion became a mass movement, and Hungarian leader Imre Nagy (pronounced "Nahj") spoke out about breaking free of the Soviet Union's control. Some Hungarians took the occasion to seek revenge against Soviet secret police, who had killed many Hungarians in

the past. Dozens of secret police were lynched. Of course, the Soviet Union was not about to tolerate such a revolt. For several days, Hungarians celebrated their new freedom. The party did not last long, however. Soviet troops and tanks soon rolled into Hungary. Many Hungarian freedom fighters tried to resist the invaders. They appealed to the United States for help. But no help came, because the Eisenhower administration did not want to risk a confrontation with the Soviet Union. In the next few days, more than twenty thousand Hungarian citizens were killed. And Imre Nagy was arrested and executed by the Soviets.

Revolution in Cuba: The Rise of Fidel Castro

Since 1956, a revolution had been occurring only ninety miles away from Key West, Florida, in the Caribbean nation of Cuba. The rebels, under the command of Fidel Castro, were fighting to overthrow the brutal and corrupt dictatorship of Fulgencio Batista. Cuba was wealthy, but the distribution of wealth was very unequal. A small group of families controlled most of the wealth of the island. The rest of the population was very poor. Batista often jailed, tortured, and murdered his political opponents. Most Cubans hated him. Castro, on the other hand, attracted followers and even had admirers in the United States. By the late 1950s, Castro and his guerrilla fighters were gaining the upper hand against Batista's troops. Finally, in January 1959, Batista fled the island. Castro and his troops entered Havana in triumph.

Once in power, Castro instituted reforms to improve the lives of the poorest Cubans. In the process, he seized private companies, including property belonging to Americans, such as sugar plantations and cattle ranches. He turned them into state-run businesses. The United States government was not pleased. It believed that Castro intended to establish communism on the island. Relations between the two countries quickly deteriorated. Ultimately, Castro would openly embrace communism, turning to the Soviet Union for economic assistance. The United States would have to learn to deal with having a Communist nation as a close neighbor.

Fidel Castro (opposite) established himself as the dictator of Cuba. After taking over American property in the island nation, Castro continued to pose a threat as an ally of the Communist Soviet Union. Over the years, the United States made several efforts to remove Castro from power, but he remains the leader of Cuba today.

The Dawn of the Computer Age

When Remington Rand introduced its UNIVAC computer in 1951, people were amazed at how "small" it was. It was fourteen by seven by nine feet, about the size of a small bedroom! Today, this seems enormous. But UNIVAC was only about one tenth of the size of earlier computers.

Throughout the 1950s, computers continued to become smaller, faster, and more powerful machines. Many businesses and academic institutions could finally afford them. Transistors replaced vacuum tubes, making the smaller machines possible. Software programs were another major innovation. The first was FORTRAN, which was used for science and mathematics. Then came COBOL, or Common Business Oriented Language, which was used for business. It was the early start of what is known today as the Information Age.

John William Mauchley (opposite left) and John Presper Eckert, Jr. (opposite right), created UNIVAC, or Universal Automatic Computer. The United States Census Bureau bought the first UNIVAC to help tabulate the results of its 1950 population count.

Sputnik (below), launched in 1957, circled Earth at eighteen thousand miles an hour, completing its orbit once every ninety-six minutes. Although it caused a scare among many Americans who feared its potential destructive power, Sputnik itself was destroyed when it fell to Earth in January 1958.

Sputnik 1 Delivers a Wake-up Call

On October 4, 1957, the Soviet Union launched *Sputnik 1*, the world's first man-made satellite, into orbit around the earth. Many Americans reacted with shock, outrage, and fear at this demonstration of Soviet superiority in space. Secretary of Defense Charles Wilson tried to calm fears by saying *Sputnik* was nothing more than a "neat scientific trick." President Eisenhower said there was nothing to worry about "as far as security is concerned." Most Americans, of course, disagreed. The United States was involved in a nuclear arms race with the Soviet Union. It now appeared likely that America's rival would soon be able to launch nuclear missiles at the United States from space. Americans were amazed that their country could have fallen so far behind the Soviet Union in rocket technology. Suddenly, government money began to pour into space research.

When the United States successfully launched its first satellite, *Explorer 1*, into orbit on January 31, 1958, Soviet leader Nikita Khrushchev had a good laugh. He pointed out that the American satellite weighed only thirty pounds, whereas the Soviets were launching satellites that weighed more than a thousand pounds. He referred to *Explorer 1* as a "little grapefruit." But America would ultimately have the last laugh when the Apollo astronauts won the space race by walking on the surface of the moon a decade later.

The United States made its move in the space race when it launched Explorer 1 *(opposite) as an answer to the Soviet satellite Sputnik.*

Swiss biochemist Friedrich Miescher had discovered DNA in 1868, but it was not until the 1950s that scientists learned about its structure or how it works. Watson and Crick were the first to describe DNA as a double helix, or a structure that resembles a twisting ladder (right). In 1957, an American scientist named Arthur Kornberg made DNA in a test tube. The work of these scientists led to the complex research now being done in biogenetics.

Determining the Structure of DNA

Scientists were also involved in work outside the space race. They were making great progress in learning how the human body works. Genes within the DNA (deoxyribonucleic acid) in the nucleus of each of our cells carry the code for manufacturing the various proteins that allow the cells to

EXPLORER 1

AMERICA'S FIRST EARTH SATELLITE

jpl

JET PROPULSION LABORATORY

CALIFORNIA INSTITUTE OF TECHNOLOGY

function. Until the 1950s, very little was known about the structure of DNA and how genes function.

In the early 1950s, Rosalind Franklin used an X-ray photographic technique to determine that DNA is helical, or spiral, in form. Then, in 1953, American biologist James Watson worked with English biophysicist Francis Crick to discover that DNA is formed by two helixes wound around each other. They then found that the double helix could unwind to allow the structure to duplicate itself exactly. These discoveries would lead to breakthroughs in the study of the genetic code on which all life is based, and an understanding of which genes are responsible for certain characteristics in human beings.

The Man Who Conquered Polio

Epidemics of polio, often referred to as "infantile paralysis," had long occurred in many parts of the world, including the United States, Europe, and Asia. A particularly severe outbreak of the disease had begun in the United States in 1942 and continued into the 1950s. In 1950 alone there were some thirty-three thousand reported cases.

Jonas Salk, an American research scientist, had begun working in 1947 to find a way to prevent the crippling disease. After several years of painstaking work in his laboratory, Salk found that, by injecting a killed poliovirus into a person, the body could build up an immunity to stronger forms of the virus. He developed a polio vaccine and proved it was safe by testing it on himself, his wife, and his children.

In 1954, more than 1.8 million schoolchildren were injected with the vaccine. In 1955, the vaccine was declared safe and effective in preventing polio. A serious disease had been conquered by a man of science.

For decades, polio was a terrible threat to people all over the world. It could not only kill, but could leave its victims paralyzed. President Franklin Delano Roosevelt was one of many stricken by the disease. Although few Americans realized the president's condition, because there was no live television at that time, Roosevelt could not stand without assistance. When a vaccine was created in the 1950s, Americans eagerly went for immunizations (opposite), hoping to avoid devastating polio epidemics in the future.

An Amazing Decade

The 1950s were a time of great prosperity for many Americans, as well as a period of contrast and change. Middle-class families were doing well in the years after World War II. Millions of children were being born, and families who could afford it were fulfilling dreams of home ownership in the suburbs. Television portrayed middle-class life as an ideal. Americans huddled together to watch their favorite television stars live wonderful lives in an idealized, fictitious suburban world.

At the same time, Americans were often huddling not around the television, but in fear. The tense years of the Cold War, the arms race, and Senator McCarthy's hunt for Communists caused people to fear a nuclear war could occur at any time. Even children, who took part in duck-and-cover drills and watched their families build fallout shelters, felt this overwhelming apprehension. Others had different fears. African Americans feared racist violence as they struggled to win the civil rights denied them for so long.

The 1950s were marked by all of these ups and downs. From the terror caused by *Sputnik* to the birth of rock 'n' roll, from the war in Korea to the poodle skirt, the 1950s were truly a unique and amazing decade.

The 1950s were a time of war, peace, and prosperity. Although Americans were involved once again in combat overseas as they tried to contain communism, they were also enjoying a booming postwar economy at home. It was the age of the birth of rock 'n' roll, which would forever change the world of music (opposite, teens dance on the hit show American Bandstand). It was also a time of conservatism that would lead to rebellion among the younger generations in later decades. The 1950s were also notable as the starting point of the civil rights movement, led by Dr. Martin Luther King, Jr. (below), which would profoundly shape the future of the United States.

1950—Christian Dior's "New Look" is the height of fashion; Ben Hogan wins the United States Open golf tournament; Joseph McCarthy announces that he has a list of Communists working in the State Department, beginning the McCarthy Red Scare; Ethel and Julius (left) Rosenberg are arrested for espionage; North Korea invades South Korea, beginning the Korean War.

1951—J. D. Salinger publishes *Catcher in the Rye*; The Rosenbergs are convicted of espionage; President Harry Truman fires General Douglas MacArthur (left); UNIVAC computer is introduced.

1952—Rocky Marciano first wins world heavyweight title; Dwight D. Eisenhower is elected president on the Republican ticket.

1953—Movies *War of the Worlds*, *House of Wax*, and *It Came from Outer Space* released; Marilyn Monroe (left) stars in *Gentlemen Prefer Blondes* and *How to Marry a Millionaire*; Ben Hogan becomes Associated Press Male Athlete of the Year; The Rosenbergs die in the electric chair; Armistice signed in the Korean War; Eisenhower administration establishes Department of Health, Education, and Welfare; Soviet leader Joseph Stalin dies; Scientists James Watson and Francis Crick discover the structure and function of DNA.

1954—Marlon Brando stars in *The Wild One*; *Creature from the Black Lagoon* released; Army-McCarthy hearings take place, with the help of McCarthy aide Roy Cohn (left); United States Supreme Court hands down its *Brown* v. *Board of Education* decision.

1955—*Rebel Without a Cause* opens in theaters; *The Blackboard Jungle* draws attention to gang-related violence in New York City; Brooklyn Dodgers defeat the New York Yankees in the World Series; Rosa Parks inspires African-American leaders, including Martin Luther King (right), to start the Montgomery Bus Boycott; Jonas Salk's polio vaccine is declared safe and effective.

1956—Congress passes the National Defense Highway Act to build more highways for defense and recreational driving; Film *Invasion of the Body Snatchers* becomes a hit; *The Ten Commandments* opens in theaters; Rocky Marciano retires from professional boxing; Dwight Eisenhower (right) is reelected president; United States Supreme Court declares bus segregation laws in Montgomery, Alabama, unconstitutional; Nikita Khrushchev becomes leader of Soviet Union; Hungary attempts to revolt against Soviet control.

1957—Jack Kerouac publishes *On the Road*; Brooklyn Dodgers move at the end of the baseball season to become the Los Angeles Dodgers; Althea Gibson becomes the first black person to win Wimbledon and the United States Open singles tennis titles; Senator Joseph McCarthy dies; First civil rights act since Reconstruction is passed; President Eisenhower sends troops to help integrate Little Rock's Central High School (right); Soviet Union launches *Sputnik 1*.

1958—Althea Gibson (bottom right), for the second consecutive year, wins Wimbledon and United States Open singles titles; United States launches *Explorer 1*; The Hula Hoop is introduced.

1959—Film *Ben-Hur* opens in theaters; Marilyn Monroe appears in *Some Like It Hot*; Fidel Castro succeeds in ousting Cuban dictator Fulgencio Batista and becomes the dictator of Cuba.

Books

Duden, Jane. *1950s*. Parsippany, N.J.: Silver Burdett Press, 1989.

Evans, Harold. *The American Century*. New York: Alfred A. Knopf, 1998.

Jennings, Peter, and Todd Brewster. *The Century*. New York: Doubleday, 1998.

Junior Chronicle of the 20th Century. New York: DK Publishing, 1997.

Kallen, Stuart A. *The 1950s*. San Diego, Calif.: Greenhaven Press, 1998.

Stein, R. Conrad. *The Korean War: "The Forgotten War."* Hillside, N.J.: Enslow Publishers, Inc., 1994.

Zeinert, Karen. *McCarthy and the Fear of Communism in American History*. Springfield, N.J.: Enslow Publishers, Inc., 1998.

Internet Addresses

Cold War Museum. September 29, 1998. <http://www.coldwar.org/>.

Korean War Project. 2000. <http://www.koreanwar.org/index.html>.

Linder, Doug. "Famous American Trials: Rosenbergs Trial, 1951." *Famous Trials*. n.d. <http://www.law.umkc.edu/faculty/projects/ftrials/rosenb/ROSENB.HTM>.

Sherlock, Joseph M. *Welcome to the Fifties*. April 2, 2000. <http://www.joesherlock.com/fifties.html>.